RUSTIC Elegance

RUSTIC
Elegance

Written and Photographed by
Ralph Kylloe

GIBBS SMITH
TO ENRICH AND INSPIRE HUMANKIND

First Edition
14 13 12 11 10   5 4 3 2 1

Text © 2010 by Ralph Kylloe
Illustrations © 2010 by Larry Pearson
Photographs © 2010 by Ralph Kylloe

Published by
Gibbs Smith
P.O. Box 667
Layton, Utah 84041

1.800.835.4993 orders
www.gibbs-smith.com

Designed by Melissa Dymock
Printed and bound in China
Gibbs Smith books are printed on either recycled, 100% post-consumer waste, FSC-certified papers or on paper produced from a 100% certified sustainable forest/controlled wood source.

Library of Congress Cataloging-in-Publication Data

Kylloe, Ralph R.
  Rustic elegance / written and photographed
by Ralph Kylloe. — 1st ed.
     p. cm.
  ISBN-13: 978-1-4236-0549-2
  ISBN-10: 1-4236-0549-7
  1. Pearson, Larry E.—Themes, motives. 2.
Country homes—United States. I. Title.
  NA737.P363K95 2010
  728'.37092—dc22
                          2010012465

Dedication

The American intelligence community discovered that the country was about to be attacked by a foreign super power. It was a serious threat. Two messengers were sent to alert the American defenses. Mr. William Dawes, one of the two messengers, traveled fast and hard throughout the night. He bravely alerted the defenders of freedom and passed the message of the impending attack throughout the network established by his superiors. In the morning the American forces, ready and organized, routed the attacking foreign super power in a fierce and bloody battle.

It is interesting to note that the other messenger sent out to inform the citizens of America on that fateful night was none other than Paul Revere. It is also interesting to note that it was Paul Revere who received the glory and fame for his efforts to muster the troops. William Dawes was quickly forgotten and his name, even though he rode just as hard and as fast as Paul Revere, was quickly lost in the quagmire of history. With that said, Dawes did fully exhibit all the qualities of true heroism.

And, so, I dedicate this book to the heroism in all of us. Most of us will never be acknowledged or recognized. Most of us will never receive fame and fortune. At the very least life can be troublesome, difficult and challenging. Many of us would rather go fishing than go to work. But we do so to support our families and ourselves. Most of us work all of our lives and endure hardships that can try the souls of even the hardiest of humans. In our own small way we are heroes all. It's a good thing to keep this in mind.

Contents

Preface

Many people ask how I find the homes I photograph. That's not at all a problem. Every architect, designer, furniture builder, contractor and decorator in the entire world wants and needs to be published. It's incredibly important to the health and growth of any business. Consequently, I'm often inundated with PR packages from business people all over the world. Sometimes I receive half a dozen packages a day from different designers wanting me to see their work. And, frankly, I love seeing new material. But I can't choose everyone, so I have to be very selective.

In truth, thousands of log cabins are constructed each year and each of them offers something unique. I chose homes for this book that were innovative. Many rustic homes today are furnished with extraordinary

traditional rustic furniture. In all honesty, every inch in both of my homes is filled with some sort of rustic furniture and rustic accessories. But for this book I wanted to show how rustic homes look with something other than rustic furniture. Consequently, the homes contained in this book feature a wide variety of furnishings, including modern, Arts and Crafts, European and other eclectic styles. But there's more to it than that. Many of the homes I've looked at and photographed lately are monastic in appearance. In other words, they are not over-burdened with accessories and furniture. Homes decorated in a simple style are often more relaxing and more intimate than those with excessive furnishings and accessories. Simplicity often has a calming effect. Further, less stuff in a home allows the visitor to appreciate the architecture and the few items that are part of the setting.

One of the more delightful innovations in interior design (it's not really an innovation; it's been around a long time but seems to be in favor at the moment) is textured walls. An extra layer of plaster is applied on top of Sheetrock. The plaster is left to dry with a rough, textured surface. Paint is then applied. Once dry, a glazing compound is applied to the surface, adding depth and character. The walls then take on an old-world appearance, sort of like a Tuscan villa or a Southwestern adobe compound. Frankly, I love it and have done this to a few walls in my own home. But for a photographer it poses some subtle problems. Sometimes dark "smudges" appear on the images and there is great inclination to remove these "aberrations" from the photograph in Photoshop. But reason prevails and I recognize this as part of the charm of the home. I just hope that no one thinks that I didn't clean my lens before making the photographs.

So, the homes offered in this book are paragons of uniqueness and character. I think the homes shown here are on the cutting edge of rustic design. They are places that I enjoyed spending time at and hated to leave when my work was done!

ACKNOWLEDGMENTS

With all of that said, I'm compelled to offer my profound thanks to many people, including Larry Pearson himself. I could go on and on about him but I think a simple "thank you" will do.

I also want to mention my editor, Madge Baird, at Gibbs Smith. Madge is the absolute sweetheart of all editors and I greatly appreciate her prodigious efforts to clean up my work and keep me from losing my mind, which, on many occasions, has nearly happened!

I also need to thank a group of individuals who helped style my photos when I visited the homes. These stylists "fluff" the pillows, arrange the flowers, build the fires in the fireplaces, organize the kitchens and make my life easy. So, a sincere "many thanks" to Eleana Montoya and Rain Turrell from the Pearson Design Group. These ladies are fun-loving, professional design people that have the ability to turn just about anything into art. Also, a special thanks to designers Bill Peace and Hillary Linthicum, with whom I've worked on many occasions.

Thanks also to Michele and Lindsey Kylloe (my wife and eleven-year-old daughter), who have styled photos on many occasions and always make my work better than it was. I also thank them for allowing me to virtually disappear in my study and work for hours, days, weeks and months on these projects.

I also need to thank my good friend Norman Van Diest. He is the mother of all computer wizards and has solved more problems for me than I can remember.

Special thanks to architect Keith Anderson from the office of PDG. Julia Miller from the PDG office was invaluable as she professionally arranged my hectic schedule and organized tons of information for me. Robert Esperti was also incredibly helpful with his ongoing mentoring and encouragement. (Bob, you're the best!) Dennis Durham was also helpful, offering insights on each project I photographed. Chris Lohss of Chris Lohss Construction was gracious in providing access to the different projects he completed that are featured in this book.

Thanks to Betsy Swartz for the artwork that hangs in many of the homes we photographed; to Kevin Hanly, Carly Gates, Carol Lehmann, Justin Tollefson, Greg Matthews, Joshua Barr, Jed Thomas, Patrick Johanson, Ben Kennedy, Nathan Crane, Alyssa Ruffie, Jacque Spitler, Carole Young, Hilary Heminway, Elizabeth Schultz, Catherine Lane, Charles De Lisle, Carole Hamill, Will Callahan and many others.

I am certain to have overlooked some individuals that should be acknowledged, and for that I apologize. Please feel free to e-mail me if I have inadvertently and thoughtlessly failed to mention an individual who was associated with the homes included in this book. I'll do my best to include such individuals in future printings.

With that said, I can't say thanks enough to the owners of the homes. You have all been gracious beyond belief. If any of you would like me to visit again during fly-fishing season, just let me know, 'cause I'll be there in a minute; and if I stay longer than a month, I promise to pay rent!

As a rule, I never say where these homes are located or mention the names of their owners. These are private homes not open to the public. Unfortunately, they are not open for viewing, casual visits, tours, cocktails, sleepovers, parties, reunions, bacchanalias, dinners, lunches, conferences, weekend happenings, or gatherings of any sort.

THE EYES OF AN *Artist*

He goes by the professional title of architect, but he's really an artist. I mention this because there are many professionals out there, but few have elevated their work to the level of the artistic. Art is a funny thing. It's a feeling. Words do not adequately describe it, but we know it when we see it. Larry Pearson lives it and breathes it. Whether he's designing a home or admiring a landscape or enjoying a dinner, Pearson gets it.

I've spent more than thirty years in the rustic design business and have written more than twenty books on the subject. I really have seen thousands of rustic homes. Nearly a decade ago, different friends encouraged me to meet architect Larry Pearson. So I called him and we agreed to meet at one of his projects near the Big Hole River in Montana. The first building

he showed me was a recently completed home called Running Water. Made completely of locally found, indigenous stones, the building, for lack of a better term, "knocked me out." The design was extraordinary, the craftsmanship superb and the ambiance was nothing less than magical. Running Water and several other Pearson homes appeared in my 2006 book *The Rustic Home*. Pearson's work has also appeared in at least four of my other books since.

At this point I know Larry fairly well. I've spent hundreds of hours with him and seen dozens of his projects from start to finish. His designs have evolved beautifully throughout the years. In truth, he's not a normal guy. I really mean this. He's the sort of person that you want to walk up to and hug. His enthusiasm is infectious. He both tutors and encourages those around him.

Pearson has a large office where he's surrounded by talent. His office is a blue jeans kind of a place. Most of the time Larry walks around the office shoeless. The door to his personal office is almost always open. His work setting is a bastion of creativity. People who work there love it. Great art happens there. He frequently draws or "doodles" on napkins or other scraps at hand. And on many occasions I've seen him chuckle to himself as he sits alone with a pencil and paper, lost in blissful thought. He sincerely loves his work.

Larry's work ethic is non-compromising. He's also a passionate, attentive listener. He pioneered a philosophy called "client-centered architecture." In an era when many people, including architects and interior designers, value their own tastes and personalities above their clients', Pearson's driving ambition is to carefully listen to and exceed his clients' expectations. At the same time, he says, the architectural process is an educational experience for both the client and himself as they learn from each other. He strives to demystify the architectural experience by both educating and involving his clients in the design of their homes. His assuring nature gives people permission to do something different.

As have all artists, Larry Pearson has been inspired by the work of other people in his field. Certainly one influence was the Swiss architect Le Corbusier. Pearson took great delight in the unconventional spirit and innovative approach of this architect of the early to mid-1900s. Other architects of note were also inspirational, including Frank Lloyd Wright and the Greene and Greene brothers, as well as the whole philosophy of the Arts and Crafts movement. At the same time, the stunning, rugged architecture of Yellowstone, Glacier and other national parks continue to inspire and influence his work.

Pearson is best known for his design of stunning rustic homes. Not only has he designed superb examples in Montana, but he has also completed extraordinary projects in Connecticut, Minnesota, Wyoming, and Canada. But his passion for architecture is not limited to rustic endeavors. His innovative projects have adapted styles of the classic South African "Cape May," Arts and Crafts, Mission, Cape Cod, Scandinavian, and what I call the ultra-modern "George Jetson" look. Each of his projects tells a story. The designs offer a continuous flow of experiences. Subtle effects and detail deliver richness and character.

But a great composer is only as good as the musicians that play the scores. Pearson surrounds himself with talent. From the masons, carpenters, lighting specialists, painters, roofers, interior designers, landscapers and a host of others, each individual working on a Pearson project is a talented artist. Together, they play great music.

I've photographed fifty or so of Larry Pearson's projects. Whenever I visit a new one I honestly feel a profound sense of well-being, awe and gratitude. Great art does that to me. His clients feel so as well.

High ENCAMPMENT

The owners of High Encampment, as the home is called, sought property with dramatic views and scenery. Once they had found their dream site, they engaged architect Larry Pearson to design an eighty-eight hundred square-foot structure. The couple sought a rustic home with rich details and expansive windows that would allow light to bathe the building.

The home includes five bedrooms as well as a covered walkway to a detached garage. They wanted a small guest cabin on the property as well.

Pearson designed a segmented home that offers a sequence of experiences. Around each corner or down any hallway is another surprise. One enters the property and drives up an incline. Little by little the drama of the home becomes apparent. Upon entering the front door, visitors climb

PREVIOUS OVERLEAF, LEFT: Upon entering the complex, the views offered at the site become apparent. A major ski resort is in the background and dark skies prepare to deposit the first snow fall in October.

PREVIOUS OVERLEAF, RIGHT: The home offers three levels as well as a second-floor porch complete with rustic railing and massive pillars. Siding materials are both rough-cut wooden planks and log.

LEFT: The front door is custom, complete with hand-forged hardware. An Arts and Crafts wall sconce lights the way.

a few steps to a rustic foyer complete with a fireplace and benches. Up another flight, a formal dining room offers another fireplace and stunning views. From there another small flight of stairs ascends to the great room complete with vaulted ceilings, fireplaces and a grand piano.

The creative folks at On Site Management were responsible for the construction of the home. The building is conventionally framed, with siding made from dead standing logs applied to both the interior and exterior of the home. The main building was engineered by Bridger Engineering. Harlowton sandstone was used for the rock work, including the chimney systems throughout the building. Elizabeth Schultz of Bozeman, Montana, served as the interior designer.

An unusual front entryway offers a fireplace and built-in bench. Staircases lead upstairs and downstairs.

ABOVE: The first landing above the entryway foyer includes the formal dining room and a row of windows to watch the bears, elk and falling snow. The dining table was completed by the creative cabinetmakers at OSM. An Arts and Crafts chandelier lights the dining table.

FACING: Just behind the dining table this massive fireplace occasionally roars with a fire and other times offers the charm of burning candles. The soft, subtle colors on the dining chairs blend well with the surroundings.

ABOVE: Media screens are accessible in different rooms.

RIGHT: A simple touch of a button commands a large flat-screen TV to ascend from below. Tim Groth created the armchairs and entertainment center.

FACING: A western-motif print rests above a Stickley spindle Morris chair and ottoman in a corner of the great room.

LEFT: The interior of the home showcases extensive Arts and Crafts detailing in the furniture, lighting and accessories. A grand piano sits in the background.

FACING: A front view of the great room shows the massive fireplace as well as the Arts and Crafts detailing.

FACING: The kitchen offers leather armchairs and a breakfast nook for quick meals before a busy day on the slopes.

RIGHT: The countertops adjacent to the industrial stove are made from soapstone. Backsplash tiles counterbalance the darkness of the wood. The pulls on the custom cabinets are reminiscent of hardware from the 1920s.

LEFT: The creative use of the many forms inherent in recycled materials is demonstrated here. The angled and contoured door leads to the pantry. The richness and character of historic materials is evident and greatly adds to the uniqueness of the setting.

FACING: A subtle chandelier created from an antique barn beam and Arts and Crafts lanterns hangs over the kitchen island. The entire island was made from recycled barn beams. The color of the leather upholstery on the bar stools picks up color from the flooring.

FACING: The master suite boasts a fireplace and Arts and Crafts lighting and well as a built-in desk with applied twig front.

ABOVE: A colorful king-size bed in a country style completes the setting.

LEFT: The master bath offers not only showers but a soaking tub raised on barn beams. The countertops on the vanities are marble. Recycled barn boards serve as flooring throughout most of the home.

BELOW: The bath just off the bunk room offers a three-faucet washbasin of cast iron.

ABOVE: A custom king bed made from historic materials anchors a guest room. A bench attached to the footboard is ideal for dressing in the morning.

RIGHT: The bunk room is a favorite place for kids of all ages. Made from recycled beams, the room is warm and inviting.

ABOVE: Another bedroom offers a four-poster canopy bed made from iron. Bed drapes slide easily and can be closed for a bit of privacy.

FACING: The colors inherent in this setting reflect a sense of calmness and relaxation. An antique iron bed, complete with subtly colored coverings and pillows, welcomes guests to the home.

FACING: The downstairs recreation room has a pool table and relaxing, oversized furniture. A large TV is hidden behind the doors on the wall, opposite the armchairs and couch.

ABOVE: A view out the ground-floor back door reveals one of the many rustic elements and a grand view of the countryside.

RIGHT: The covered breezeway to the garage includes this dramatic column of tree trunk pillars and Arts and Crafts lighting.

ABOVE: High Encampment offers dramatic views of the nearby ski slopes and mountains. The outdoor fireplace and picnic station are used during every season, to the delight of the kids and guests.

FACING: A late spring snowfall brightens the colors of the recycled materials on the exterior of the home.

CUTTHROAT *Cabin*

The owners of High Encampment also wanted a small guest cabin on their property. Offering less than a thousand feet of living space, the cabin sits a few hundred feet from the main building, near a stream and trout pond. Reflecting the historic homestead buildings of the West, this cabin, built by OSM, appears to have been in the same spot for generations. On this particular day of photographing, I was startled by a deer and fawn that were less than ten feet from my tripod. I could have reached out and pet the fawn, but didn't. The following day I hurried back to my vehicle when a black bear, just twenty yards from me, wandered up to the pond, took a few sips and spent an hour or so digging in the grass. I have photographed this home on several occasions and been tempted to toss a few flies with my fly rod into the pond, as fish seem to rise throughout the day. Lacking the owner's permission, I refrained.

PREVIOUS OVERLEAF, LEFT: This small building, called Cutthroat Cabin, serves as guest quarters for High Encampment, whose main building is a few hundred feet away. The cabin has a shake shingle roof, log siding and a massive fireplace.

PREVIOUS OVERLEAF, RIGHT: Located on the slopes of a major Rocky Mountain ski resort guests are invited, in the winter time only, to ski right out their front door!

ABOVE: The living room in the cabin offers Craftsman-style furniture, a leather couch, a twig rocker and an Oriental carpet.

LEFT: A ladder leads up to a small balcony in the cabin. The built-in benches and dining table are shown in the background. An oriental throw rug adds distinction to the room.

ABOVE: A massive fireplace sits off of the kitchen and living room.

RIGHT: The kitchen offers built-in cabinets and rustic rafters in the ceiling. The Kazak carpet adds depth to the room. A small Aga range fits perfectly into the wall of stone. The subtle green tiles behind the stove complement the setting.

ABOVE: The master bedroom in the cabin is complete with a king-size bed and an Arts and Crafts chandelier. Windows on two walls let in ample daylight.

FACING: The bunk room in the cabin is complete with this organic bunk bed and a variety of colors and textiles.

FACING: A two-faucet cast-iron sink sits in the bathroom of the guesthouse.
Birch bark–covered doors front a vanity with wood slab countertops.

ABOVE: A small soaking tub resting on barn beam feet occupies the bathroom.

DOUBLE D *Ranch*

I had featured the owners' guest camp in my book *The Rustic Cabin.* It was, and still is, a spectacular place. So, when I was told about the Double D Ranch, I was certain that I had already photographed the building. Throwing caution to the wind, on a cold and rainy day, with questions heavy on my mind, I followed my styling assistants, Rain Turrell and Eleana Montoya, to the property. The directions were the same, the roads and the scenery were the same and the entrance to the property was the same. Nonetheless, a new house had sprung up on the grounds and I was thrilled to see such a structure.

Overlooking a major river, the view from the site was spectacular. In truth, I had fished the river below the home on many occasions and had

PREVIOUS OVERLEAF: Approaching from the north, the full scale of the structure becomes visible. Offering three separate chimney systems, the home consists of seventy-five hundred square feet of living space. The roof is covered with a combination of shake shingles and cold rolled steel.

ABOVE: The Double D Ranch on a cold and rainy fall day. From the southern view, this home appears subtle and unassuming. The two-vehicle garage on the left includes an upstairs guest apartment.

FACING: A floral arrangement in an iron stand anchors in the corner of the entry hallway.

been told by many people to avoid the bluffs that rose before me because of the high concentration of rattlesnakes. I took their advice to heart and never ventured beyond the shores of the river. Once we were at the home I was again cautioned to be careful when wandering around outside because of the (gulp) rattlesnakes.

That said, this home is a clear statement of both interior and exterior innovation. Although the structure is rustic, the interior design of the building is, please excuse me for saying this, not at all what I expected. In fact, it exudes a truly fresh way of approaching the décor of a rustic home.

The architecture is what I have come to expect from Larry Pearson. The staggered roofline offers several different levels. The form of the home "flows" and is well balanced. The textures of the different materials used in the setting offer richness and character and blend this building well with the environment.

The owners had dreamed of a Western home all of their lives. They built the home themselves, with the help of a few subcontractors. The owners wrote to me and said, "The design of the home was from the extraordinary talents and efforts of Larry Pearson. The process was effortless, engaging, and Larry 'nailed' the owners' desire the first time around." In all honesty, these are the exact sentiments shared with me by the owners of the other homes built by Pearson that I've photographed over the years.

The homeowner also spoke very highly of Jeanne Jenkins of Secret Garden Interiors, who was responsible for the interior design.

LEFT: Graceful barstools line the counter, while a pair of tall cowboy and cowgirl bronzes stand watch.

FACING: An opposing view of the kitchen shows the front of the island. A large cabinet on the far wall provides shelving for china and other dining/kitchen items.

FACING: The custom kitchen sink and cabinets reflect a European flavor. The countertop is marble. The window treatment is a rich fabric swag.

ABOVE: A stone shelf by a small kitchen window provides space for country collectibles and accessories.

RIGHT: The stone wall has a recessed area for the range and side cabinets. The tiles above the stove do not compete with, but rather complement, the eclectic mix of colors and forms in the setting.

LEFT: A colorful cabinet serves as kitchen storage and a display space for collectibles.

FACING: A side view of the kitchen shows the mixing of different colors, textures and forms. The countertop on the island is marble.

LEFT: The lengthy dining table, decorated for the fall season, hosts a number of upholstered chairs and awaits guests for dinner. Many of the antique lighting fixtures throughout the home were acquired from salvage companies around the country.

FACING: The colors and variety of furnishings reflect an eclectic mix of European styles and designs. As in many homes, the kitchen is the hub of the household here, with a network of ceiling rafters and a back wall of stone reinforcing the old-world feel.

FACING: The family room off the kitchen area offers seating with floral upholstery, a European-influenced coffee table with partial leather top, and lighting of different styles.

RIGHT: Another view of the family room shows the extensive use of floral patterns in the window treatments, pillows, upholstery and rug.

ABOVE: An overview of the family sitting room shows oversized leather
chairs and other furniture pieces arranged in conversation groups.

FACING: An asymmetrical arrangement on the mantel in the family
room is made of an interesting collection of natural materials.

FACING: The library is located just off the kitchen. Built-in shelves with a movable ladder occupy one complete wall. A pair of French-influenced armchairs with Federal ticking upholstery rest on either side of a table covered with a floor-length cloth.

RIGHT: With its floral wallpaper, balloon window shades and decorative lights, this office exudes an elegant country appeal.

LEFT: The ambiance here is certainly not typical of a rustic setting. Nonetheless, this painted cottage bed with dramatic crown canopy is quite inviting. The rich multilayered approach involving different textiles and colors is an innovative approach to rustic design.

FACING: A pair of unique 1920s armchairs, an Art Nouveau boudoir table lamp, a richly upholstered ottoman and plenty of rich fabrics create a comfortable bedroom corner. Under the ottoman is an authentic cowhide to boot!

LEFT: The opposing wall of the master bath shows a continuation of the interior scheme for the room. An exquisitely upholstered ottoman is ideal for dressing, while the antique crystal chandelier brings a graceful addition to the room.

FACING: The large master bath is layered with texture and color.

FACING: The "Cowgirl Suite" offers a gas fireplace and built-in window seat. The base of the window seat pulls out and turns into a trundle bed for infant cowboys and cowgirls.

RIGHT, ABOVE: The Cowgirl Suite features a 1920s brass and iron bed complete with a crown canopy and luxurious fabrics. An Art Nouveau cabinet with doors and drawers provides storage space.

RIGHT, BELOW: The old-style dial/push-button phone really works and is appropriate in its setting of red colors and fancy fabrics!

FACING: Family photos and a gorgeous floral arrangement in an old cowboy boot rest on top of this bureau.

RIGHT: The "Cowgirl Bath," the owner freely admits, has a bordello appearance. Raised sinks rest on a granite countertop. This is a setting to spur the imagination!

LEFT AND FACING: The "Wolf Room" offers this unique bed built by the hands of the owner's father. A family tree is carved into the headboard and additions are made as the family grows. Trompe l'oeil paintings of bricks make the walls look old. Pillows, a bolster and rich fabrics enhance the ambiance of the room.

LEFT: The "Moose Room" proffers bunks for tired cowboys.

FACING: A room above the garage offers guests some private time when visiting D & D Ranch. A sleigh bed, chaise lounge and a desk for writing make this a comfortable place for resting or, heaven forbid, working.

FACING: This continental bureau was fashioned into a vanity complete with copper-colored fixtures and a hammered-copper sink. The textured walls offer a number of artistic renditions.

ABOVE: This bath offers a cast-iron sink with three faucets. Four layered lanterns provide ample light.

RIGHT: The vanity in this particular bathroom offers an antique copper sink where cowboys and cowgirls can refresh themselves after spending time in the D & D Saloon.

FACING: The "D & D Saloon," as it is known, boasts a vintage bar purchased in Savannah, Georgia. The custom back of the bar is fitted with a hidden karaoke screen to help struggling singers with the words to songs. Bordello red colors are in keeping with the theme of the Old West!

ABOVE: The D & D Saloon has a stage, where guitars wait in ready for an evening's entertainment.

FACING: A large fireplace anchors the other end of the recreation room. And in between is comfortable seating in stylish western theme. The many pillows on the sofa add to the depth or layered look of the setting. An exercise room (partially visible on the left) offers the family a place to work out after a hard day of chasing rattlesnakes!

RIGHT: Just off the recreation room and sitting on top of a room-size Heriz carpet is this high-style antique pool table and necessary accompanying furniture.

Mirror
POND CABIN

I had driven past the lot several times over the years. It was very high in the mountains and getting there in the winter was, at the very least, troublesome. Frankly, how anyone could build a home on the site was beyond me. Then, one spring day, I was touring the area with Larry Pearson when we pulled onto a newly created (albeit muddy) driveway on the very site I had passed many times. I was happy we had a four-wheel drive vehicle. At the end of the driveway, to my shock and surprise, stood Mirror Pond Cabin (I still struggle calling this home a "cabin") on that very site.

The first time I saw the building it was under construction. It was, no doubt, a massive undertaking. Workmen were everywhere. Cranes, bulldozers, cement trucks, sawhorses, mountains of building material and pickup

trucks occupied every inch of available space. Mud was everywhere as well. It was not a pretty site and I will admit that it took a certain amount of "vision" to realize the potential inherent in the project.

What first amazed me was the size and scope of the venture. The boulders and rocks used for the fireplace and other structural places were enormous. I was certain that each piece weighed several tons. Walking among the rocks I had no idea how humans could move such heavy material. The men on scaffolds high above the ground really did look like ants as they worked to set each massive stone in place. But if the pyramids were built without the use of machines, then I was certain that

the men before me, who had cranes and power machines of all sorts, could handle this job.

And the logs were no different. Massive in every way, moving them and placing them in position would be no easy task.

The interior of the home, which is 11,000 square feet, appeared even more chaotic. Materials of all sorts, miles of wiring and dust enough to clog the nostrils of an elephant, seemed more like a disaster zone than the portent to an artistic monument. Stacks of dusty architectural drawings were the guidelines for things to come. Personally, considering that there were all kinds of scribblings on the plans, I had no idea how such a project could come to fruition from the blueprints I held in my hands.

PREVIOUS OVERLEAF, LEFT: Massive in every way, the home occupies a southern view of the Rocky Mountains. Complete with ski in/ski out accessibility, the home is used year-round. The many levels of the structure are indicative of a complex yet inviting design. Also apparent is the multi-textural façade of the building, adding to its character. The property has a main building and a fire tower guest wing complete with an indoor parking facility for numerous vehicles, all connected by a rustic breezeway. There is also a great pond out back for ice skating in winter (which seems to be most of the year) or skinny-dipping on warm evenings. But look out for the elk and bear that often visit the property!

PREVIOUS OVERLEAF, RIGHT: The building was engineered to withstand significant seismic activity and ten-foot snow loads. The home offers an ongoing experience of interrelated geometric design.

FACING: Numerous rustic elements, including banisters, railing systems and rafters, add to the overall rustic ambiance of the setting.

RIGHT: The geometric design of the entire home is consistent and remarkably well balanced. This chimney uses a "soldier course" on the top row of stones. The stone material throughout the setting displays remarkable texture and character.

But, alas, I am neither a contractor nor an architect.

But with time and talent all things change. A season later the home was a monument to the talents of many people. And as I walked through the rooms I was again reminded that the human race was capable of astonishing feats.

Bridger Engineering of Bozeman, Montana, was responsible for insuring that the building would still be standing hundreds of years from now. And considering that the area averages ten feet of snow throughout the cold months (which often last until May), the structure needed to withstand hundreds of tons of snow on the roof system at any time. On Site Management Construction, also of Bozeman, were the contractors for the project. Angel Sandoval of Sandoval Masonry was responsible for the stonework throughout the home. Larry Pearson was the architect, and the interiors department at his firm, consisting of the talented Rain Turrell and Eleana Montoya, was responsible for the exceptional design and décor for the interior of the home.

LEFT: The front door, made from historic barn beams, is a massive element created by Dan Pittenger at OSM. The custom hardware adds to the rustic elegance and grandeur of the entryway.

FACING: Inside the front door is a foyer complete with grand staircase and a rustic coat rack for hanging coats or hats.

FACING: The tall, vaulted ceilings of the great room appear at the top of the staircase. The room is a mixture of many styles. The Arts and Crafts lighting was created by Gerry Rucks. A cowhide rests on the floor in front of a pair of armchairs covered with mohair.

RIGHT: The great room offers a variety of furniture styles and accessories. The drapes were fabricated and hung by John Tate of Bozeman. Mimi London was responsible for the oversized mission recliner.

FACING: A reverse angle of the great room demonstrates that a variety of fabrics and colors can and do complement each other. The incorporation of traditional furnishings and accessories into rustic homes brings about a fresh appearance and inviting approach.

ABOVE, LEFT: Soapstone is used for the kitchen sink and countertops. The cabinets were created from recycled barn boards in the cabinet shop at OSM.

ABOVE, RIGHT: The kitchen offers a built-in range with steel exhaust hood. The tiles are from Britt Studios of Big Fork, Montana. The countertop on the island is soapstone.

The dining room off the kitchen includes a massive custom dining table made by the creative cabinetmakers at OSM. The antler chandelier was fashioned by Frank Long of Bozeman.

The antique leather dining chairs are from
Montana Expressions. The rug is from the
Alanya Carpet Gallery in Bozeman, Montana.

The bar stools are of southwestern design.
The countertop is recycled pine.

LEFT: A dramatic painting from Betsy Swartz Fine Art Consulting overhangs a queen-size bed in the master bedroom. The chenille throw on the bed is by Dintiman Designs of San Francisco. The Arts and Crafts chandelier is by Gerry Rucks.

FACING: The master bedroom also contains a built-in corner fireplace.

FACING, ABOVE: The upstairs master bath offers a soaking tub, two showers, and two sinks. An upholstered ottoman is an ideal spot to dry oneself after a hot shower.

FACING, BELOW: The countertops for this vanity were created from old barn boards. The sink is granite.

RIGHT: Clean lines are indicative of the design of this home. The tub is cast iron and the faucets are nickel covered.

LEFT: A pair of light tan armchairs from Ralph Lauren occupies a family room in the fire tower guest quarters.

FACING: Influenced by the historic fire towers of the National Park System, Pearson incorporated a similar design element into the Mirror Pond property. The tower serves as guest quarters.

EL Rancho

El Rancho was easy to find. I had driven past the property where the home sits many times but was not aware of its existence. The compound is located off the road, just up the mouth of a picturesque valley in the Rocky Mountains. A bit farther on is a medium-size ski resort. Elk, bears, deer and coyotes live in the valley and surrounding mountains, and it is not uncommon for eagles to pass overhead. The site on which the home resides is a bucolic setting with dramatic views in just about all directions. With that said, in some sense, it is not a traditional rustic home. More and more owners are looking to expand the scope and vision of rustic design. But the house blends exceptionally well with the setting and, like many Larry Pearson designs, looks like it belongs there.

LEFT: A roofline view of the building exterior shows the artistic craftsmanship of the masonry on the chimney. The roof was completed with cold rolled steel. The top surface of this material rusts quickly, thus presenting a historical appearance.

FACING: The lower level seating area offers views of the surrounding mountains. The leather couch and Eastern Indian coffee table sit on top of a room-size geometric Kilim carpet from Turkey. Such carpets are made from goat hair rather than wool.

The owner of the home was willing to take risks with the project. He wanted an innovative structure for not only himself and his friends but his horses as well. It had to be a twenty-first-century approach to the project. Because of the expanse of windows, light fills the rooms. The dwelling is described as a "naked structure" because of the exposed wiring in the building's interior. The interiors can best be described as "fifties modern." Personally, I refer, in my own mind, to the residence as a "George Jetson" home. The owners were responsible for the interior design. Michael D. Casey of Authentic Montana Homes was the builder.

The building is respectful of the environment and the ecosystem. The form of the structure is basically agrarian in nature. It started out as both a granary and a barn but quickly evolved into a barn and attached apartment. The exterior colors of the building match the waves of wild grasses that cover the rolling fields and foothills just outside the front door. Trout ponds were added and wildlife is often seen drinking by the shores of the pools. I've had the opportunity on numerous occasions to spend time at the ranch. One day while walking the property I nearly gave myself a heart attack when I came within a few feet of a sleeping badger sunning himself by his den just a few hundred feet from the home. And I must also admit that temptation got the best of me and I did cast a few flies into the ponds—I caught and released several large rainbow trout!

The ranch is a comfortable, inviting home, and you can't argue with the monster trout in the ponds!

FACING: The master bedroom sits off of the ground-floor living room. Colored concrete floors and textured walls are an extension of colors found in the local environment. The closet doors are lined with frosted glass, while the platform bed with harmonious colors creates a restful setting. Geometric forms throughout the room provide a feeling of simplicity.

RIGHT: Simple geometric lines are at work here again. This lower level bedroom offers clean lines and a modern approach to rustic décor.

FACING: A spiral staircase made of steel provides access to the different levels in the home. The bottom two steps of the staircase were created from stone. Exposed track lighting runs throughout.

ABOVE AND RIGHT: The steel banister and spiral staircase are consistent with the high-tech approach to the home. The sweeping curves of the railing soften the general geometric design.

LEFT: This high-style side chair, made of chrome with a leather inset seat, fits well into the high-tech setting in the office.

FACING: A room off the main floor of the building provides space for an office, including a contemporary design desk and cabinets. A zebra skin covers part of the floor.

FACING: The kitchen area is tucked neatly into a corner, with a sofa seating area and flat-screen TV nearby. The kitchen cabinets are covered with softly frosted glass, allowing chefs to find what they are looking for with ease. The kitchen and island countertops are black honed granite.

RIGHT: The minimalist approach to the design and décor allows visitors to appreciate the architecture and objects of art throughout the home. The colorful paintings on the wall are of western influence.

House
MOUNTAIN

Seeking a traditional mountain home, the owners of House Mountain sought out architect Larry Pearson. They requested a hand-hewn exterior and a structure big enough to accommodate a large family and guests. They wanted a very large fireplace and a central meeting point for entertaining guests. A family wing complete with sleeping quarters as well as guest accommodations on the opposite end of the home were also requested. The owners allowed the architect significant freedom with the design and worked closely with him throughout the project. The result is a rather astonishing structure that greatly exceeded the expectations of the clients.

PREVIOUS OVERLEAF, LEFT: Sandoval Masonry was responsible for the stonework. The outside pillars are peeled lodgepole pine.

PREVIOUS OVERLEAF, RIGHT: Angel Sandoval and his crew of talented stonemasons created several fireplaces and extensive rockwork for the home.

LEFT: The exterior of the home is architecturally interesting with several different levels and entranceways. The season's first snowfall reminds one that firewood needs to be stacked early.

FACING: The great room is as dramatic as it is comfortable. There is often great temptation to overdo a room this size with excessive furniture and accessories. The minimalist use of furniture adds to the grandeur of the setting and prevents an overcrowding sensation often associated with too much clutter. Joe Holley created the chandelier from a Keith Anderson design. Angel Sandoval created the massive fireplace.

The sixty-four-hundred-square-foot, five-bedroom house with detached garage was constructed by OSM of Bozeman, Montana. Angel Sandoval of Sandoval Masonry was responsible for the fireplaces and stonework throughout. Davis Torres of Bozeman served as the interior design team for the project, providing much of the furniture from their gallery.

FACING: A small nook off the great room is complete with a western leather club chair and ottoman and an Arts and Crafts lamp resting on a pine table.

ABOVE: Soft, earthy colors are used throughout the home. The walls throughout are textured and glazed. A minimalist approach to the interior design includes simple but colorful accessories, furniture and window treatments.

RIGHT: Many rooms today are being painted to add color and life to a setting. Often, in a desire to bring a sense of history and warmth, an extra glaze and texture are added to the wall. This scrolled-arm chair and ottoman fit perfectly in the setting. The simple forms of the vases and table lamp complement the simplicity of the room.

LEFT: The stainless steel range is surrounded by custom cabinets made of recycled barn boards. The hood above the range is also covered with antique boards.

FACING, ABOVE: The kitchen offers a small breakfast nook made of old barn beams. The countertops are soapstone. Shades match the accent pillows and other textiles in the room.

FACING, BELOW: Western barstools, a pine sideboard and a corner fireplace complete the kitchen.

The formal dining room includes this massive table made in the cabinet shop at OSM. The chandelier was designed by Keith Anderson at PDG. The tall-back dining chairs were provided by Davis Torres. Large windows throughout most of the home allow views of the rugged outdoor scenery.

The stone used throughout the setting is sandstone from Harlowton, Montana. Recycled pine boards are utilized for the flooring.

FACING: Keith Anderson designed the chandelier. The lighting fixtures were fabricated by hand in the Joe Holley studio.

ABOVE: This dramatic staircase leads to the second floor of the family wing.

LEFT: A teepee on the second floor landing offers plenty of excitement for the kids and more than likely the guests as well!

FACING: A working corner fireplace of dry-stacked stone is a main feature of this bedroom, whose colors are subdued and restful.

ABOVE: One of the guest bedrooms offers a comfortable leather armchair as well as a colorful assortment of plants, vases, and paintings.

FACING: The upstairs loft in the family section offers this built-in hideaway sleeping station and drawers for extra storage.

RIGHT: A southwestern bed in red paint nestles into a wall nook and sits on a colorful rug.

BELOW, LEFT: The vanity was created from recycled barn boards. The cast-iron sink rests below the countertop. A classy rustic mirror dresses up the barn wood vanity.

BELOW, RIGHT: One of several bathrooms in the home contains this soaking tub, which rests on old barn beams instead of the typical iron claw feet.

FACING: This sitting room is part of the guest wing and offers comfortable furnishings in a casual, relaxing atmosphere.

RIGHT: The doors above the fireplace mantel in the guest wing open to reveal a TV.

FACING: A sitting room in the guest wing offers a leather cowhide sofa, club chair and ottoman—and skiing right out the door!

RIGHT: A western-motif floor lamp of quill, bow and arrows lights a corner of the guest sitting room.

BELOW: The staircase off the sitting room leads to the downstairs guest bedrooms and recreation areas.

LEFT: The bright colors create a playful ambiance in this guest bedroom. Folding window covers keep out the light when one needs extra sleep.

FACING: A variety of furnishings and colors create a dramatic room that welcomes guests.

FACING: The entranceway to the back porch is up a set of uneven stone stairs.

RIGHT: A single Gypsy willow chair rests by an open fire pit on the first snowy day of the year.

SKYART
Lodge

Arguably one of the most dramatic homes ever, the lodge sits on an exposed ridge at a very high elevation near the tree line. The siting of the home offers commanding views of some of the most dramatic scenery in the world. To make matters more interesting, it's a "ski-in, ski-out" structure as well. Many of Pearson's homes are incorporated into the environment so well that full, complete views of his structures are rare. However, because of the exposed nature of this site, the home is visually engaging from both the exterior and interior.

Much of this home can be seen from a distance. The driveway, however, is both winding and steep, thus allowing only partial views of

PREVIOUS OVERLEAF, LEFT: The building is sited for dramatic views of the surrounding mountains. An in-ground pool provides a reprieve on hot, dry mountain days.

PREVIOUS OVERLEAF, RIGHT: Located near the tree line, the home rests majestically in the northern Rockies.

LEFT: The many rooflines show the complexity of the structure. The roof is covered with cedar shake shingles and the exposed rafters are protected with lead flashing. The chimneys, topped with standing soldier courses, were constructed from Harlowton stone.

the structure as one approaches the complex. Once on the driveway, the first building encountered is a small, three-hundred-square-foot rustic ski house. A few hundred yards farther up the road, a charming fifteen-hundred-square-foot guesthouse and trout pond appear. Another hundred yards allows views of a carefully landscaped rock garden and an outdoor cooking area. Rumor has it that a black bear was once found taking a dip in the swimming pool just out the front door!

Entering the complex, one moves through a porte cochere and into a courtyard complete with center fountain. The left side of the courtyard offers sixteen hundred feet of housing for vehicles with an apartment above. The main building, on the right, offers nearly thirteen thousand square feet of living space, but only a small part of the main house is visible from the courtyard. However, a passionate assemblage of architectural lines and a sea of shake shingles create an awareness of the grandeur of the home.

The house is a weighty structure. Stones used throughout the building were excavated from the property. The buildings were constructed on a scree field of rock and stone, and the structures were actually "stepped" into the rock itself. The entire site had to be re-contoured to meet the needs of the design. Further, once excavation began, a spring of water appeared and was used to feed the trout pond on the mid-section of the property. Pearson describes the structure as a "pinwheel," as it engages visitors with a constant "discovery" down each hallway and at each turn. The kitchen is really the hub and the center of living. Each room in the building has at least two or three windows that make it possible for the home to be flooded with light. Further, the huge windows do the site justice by allowing incredible views to be seen from throughout the home.

The six-bedroom, three-story home was built by Chris Lohss Construction. San Francisco–based Charles de Lisle served as the interior designer for the project. The owners requested a non-traditional approach for the interiors, wanting a "found object," eclectic look as well as a departure from traditional Western themes and furnishings.

ABOVE: An assortment of ornate candlesticks makes a unique table grouping.

RIGHT: The primary living room offers an eclectic mix of styles and colors. Such an approach allows a setting to become visually exciting. Interior designer Charles de Lisle incorporated a variety of furniture styles and hues to bring life to the room.

FACING, ABOVE: The kitchen is often described as the "center of life" in a home. The cabinets, island and island countertop were created from recycled barn beams. The remaining countertop surfaces are soapstone. The hexagon tiles behind the stove and under the cabinets were inspired by an antique Victorian patchwork quilt. The contemporary metal barstools, from Antoine Proulx, blend well with the rustic setting.

FACING, BELOW: The massive dining table was constructed from a 250-year-old oak tree the owners found on their California property. The casual dining chairs are covered with Scottish wool plaid.

RIGHT: The formal dining room offers an elegant round table and upholstered side chairs. The room is lighted with a snowflake-glass chandelier from Paris, France. This chandelier was one of only two examples created from this design.

ABOVE, LEFT: Iron balusters support the wooden banister in the staircase system. An antique tavern table with spool turned legs serves as a resting place for decorative items.

ABOVE, RIGHT: A rugged custom door created from recycled beams serves as an entry to one of the six bedrooms in the home. Most of the floors throughout the structure are antique barn boards. A massive fireplace provides drama.

FACING: The master bedroom offers a pony-hide headboard. Matching glass-base table lamps illuminate both sides of the bed. Built-in drawers offer extra space under the window seat, and a flat-screen TV occupies a corner wall space. The carpet is Moroccan Berber.

FACING: One of the kids' rooms contains a pair of double beds from the La Lune Collection. An antique Turkish Oushak carpet covers the floor.

ABOVE: A tall, wooden, four-poster bed sits in front of the fireplace in this guest bedroom. A single moose antler rests on the fireplace mantel, while a contemporary painting sits above an antique bureau.

ABOVE, RIGHT: This bedroom contains a queen-size bed designed to resemble the industrial iron beds from the turn of the last century. This bed was constructed from wood. The brightly colored curtains, bureaus, carpet and comforter add life to the room.

RIGHT: A downstairs bunk room provides sleeping space for the many guests that visit.

LEFT: A three-faucet sink made of cast iron accommodates guests.

BELOW: The main bath offers a soaking tub with dramatic views. The custom cabinets were made from antique barn boards. The pulls on the cabinet doors in the bath and kitchen are in the style of country hardware from the 1920s and earlier. The sinks (there are two) are antique terra-cotta planters, and the tops for the bath and counter are granite.

FACING: Four Bar Harbor wicker armchairs surround an antique pine table in the downstairs recreation room. The fireplace mantel is an antique barn beam.

POND *Cabin*

This small, 450-square-foot cabin serves as guest quarters for Skyart Lodge. It is located a few hundred feet lower than the main building and also offers dramatic views of the nearby mountains. It's blessed with a small trout pond just outside the back door, and on any given day elk and deer, mountain goats, moose, and an occasional bear are seen enjoying the cool spring waters for either a bath or an afternoon drink!

Because of the high elevation, the cabin was engineered by Bridger Engineers to withstand ten-foot snow loads. I have driven by the cabin on many occasions when the building had nearly disappeared under heavy snowfalls.

PREVIOUS OVERLEAF: The home was constructed from dead standing lodgepole pine trees and locally quarried stones. The building offers one fireplace and sits comfortably near the tree line in the northern Rockies.

LEFT: The entry room is complete with an iron chandelier and an antique yellow church pew as seating for changing out of snow gear. Six bow-back Windsor side chairs surround a round iron-leg table used for "formal" dinners after a long day on the slopes.

FACING: A massive fireplace anchors one end of the family room, which is outfitted with an eclectic mix of country furnishings. A small iron chandelier provides illumination for the setting.

The roof was made of cold rolled steel, which rusts on top, thus allowing the building to quickly appear as a historical structure. The home, built by the talented artists at Chris Lohss Construction, was created from dead standing trees and locally quarried stones found directly on the property. The interior of the cabin was designed by Charles De Lisle of San Francisco and furnished with an eclectic flavor. It boasts a massive fireplace and sleeps at least six guests. Larry Pearson was the architect.

FACING: The kitchen island is made from recycled pine trees and rough-cut pine boards. Iron bar stools with woven leather seats and backs provide seating for the island.

RIGHT: The kitchen cabinets are created from recycled barn beams, and a new old-style gas range perpetuates an authentic country feel.

ABOVE, LEFT: A communal, three-faucet sink offers plenty of space to get cleaned up before meals!

ABOVE: The master bedroom offers a tall iron canopy bed complete with down bedding. The headboard is covered with leather. The curtains in a country checkerboard pattern and a bow-front bureau give the room a homey feel.

FACING: The bunk room sleeps four guests and is the favorite place for kids. The beds were made from lodgepole pine. A bow-back Windsor side chair provides a place to put on your slippers in the morning. Ticking material was used as bedding for the bunks.

LONE MOOSE
Lodge

Initially, a couple approached architect Larry Pearson to design a building for them. They were an active family and involved in a number of different sports and activities. They owned property and wanted a large home that would accommodate an extended family and friends. The family wanted the rugged appearance and character of a historical rustic structure for their home, one that blended well with the environment. While visiting the building site, the owners were impressed with another building under construction on an adjacent property higher up the mountain. Almost immediately they fell in love with the building that was, in reality, a spec home designed by Pearson. So rather than designing and building a completely new structure, they simply purchased the spec home.

PREVIOUS OVERLEAF, LEFT: The home has direct access to ski slopes right out a side door.

PREVIOUS OVERLEAF, RIGHT: The entry to the home begins at a lower level. A massive custom door made of recycled timbers and hand-forged hinges and related door hardware greets visitors. Artwork and accessories complete the entrance room.

LEFT: The entryway area is complete with a huge bronze moose, leather armchair and appropriate artwork.

FACING: The formal dining room sits off the kitchen and at the top of the entryway staircase. The room offers a dining set as well as custom sconces, chandeliers and vintage Navajo floor coverings.

Lone Moose Lodge offers a little more than ten thousand square feet of living space. It has seven bedrooms—one of which is a bunk room—eight and a half baths, several fireplaces and an attached three-car garage. With a bit more than two thousand square feet of outside porches, decks and terraces, including a hot tub, this is an ideal home for an active family.

The home was constructed by the folks at Chris Lohss Construction. Bill Peace and Hillary Linthicum of Peace Design served as the interior design team. The stonework was provided by the Sandoval Masonry Company. Bridger Engineering oversaw the engineering aspects of the home. Greg Matthews served as project manager from the architect's office. William Callahan of Savantage served as the owners' representative and was instrumental in organizing the different teams of tradesmen and artists to complete the project. The artwork on the walls was provided by Tierney Fine Art Gallery and Montana Trails Gallery, both of Bozeman.

LEFT: The large dining table takes a set of twelve leather side chairs. A fireplace, which is part of the main chimney system off the great room, provides warmth and ambiance for the area.

FACING, ABOVE: The kitchen offers custom cabinets and a complete "wet" island surrounded by four leather upholstered bar stools. The butcher-block island top is made of walnut. Yellow brick tiles occupy the wall behind the range and countertops. The unique chandeliers above the island are actually antique ship lights modified to serve as kitchen lighting.

FACING, BELOW: The kitchen offers both seating around the island and an upholstered breakfast nook in the corner of the room. The top on the nook table is created from recycled oak boards, while the upholstery on the bench cushions is classic southwestern style.

FACING, ABOVE: Off the kitchen is a private bar and sitting room. The chairs were created by Hancock and Moore. The countertops were made from distressed recycled materials.

FACING, BELOW: The sitting room off the kitchen offers leather and upholstered seating. The fireplace façade was created from historic barn beams and boards. Two large vintage photos of Native Americans occupy a back wall. A simple four-light chandelier offers subtle illumination for the room.

RIGHT: The chandelier above the bar is an antique Italian item from Robuck and Company Antiques. The crackled mirror behind the bar is also antique.

FACING: A small sitting room overlooks one of the nearby ski slopes and is often used as a morning coffee room by the owners and their guests. The intricate ceiling took two months to complete. Antique snowshoes and skis as well as other items add ambiance to the room.

ABOVE: An oversized leather armchair complete with spool turned legs sits off to the side of the fireplace in the great room. An original oil painting of a western scene hangs on the wall.

RIGHT: The great room shows the upholstered furniture, the massive chandelier and a unique seat made from an antique wooden saddle. The red carpet and throw pillows add energy to the setting. A floor-to-ceiling fireplace of Harlowton stone anchors the great room. A moose head hangs above the mantel. A massive metal chandelier created by Fire Mountain Forge of Livingston, Montana, lights the room.

FACING: A small sitting room off the great room offers four Molesworth-style armchairs made by Marc Taggart. A large African drum serves as a coffee table and an antler chandelier hangs from the ceiling.

RIGHT: A Native American decorative headpiece provides a textural, visual accessory to the setting.

BELOW: The top of the stairs could have been completed with just a railing, but Pearson chose to make the space functional with built-in seating and storage space.

FACING: The master bedroom offers a corner fireplace, custom rustic doors and lush drapes. A colorful Western painting rests above the mantel. An original beaver fur blanket covers the foot of the bed.

RIGHT: A custom bed and headboard designed by Formations in a classic rustic style are perfectly complemented by red window treatments and carpet. Textiles add layers to the setting.

FACING: A small study/office sits off the main bedroom. Complete with a leather sofa, a cowhide on the floor and appropriate decorative accessories, the room overlooks the ski slopes right out the back door.

RIGHT: The bunk room has a pair of massive bunk beds made from dead standing lodgepole pine. A Pendleton blanket continues the western theme expressed throughout the home.

ABOVE: Yet another bedroom offers this unique bed complete with southwestern-style headboard and quilted bedding. The patchwork carpet complements the geometric setting of the home.

FACING: An upholstered sleigh bed is complete with thick bedding and stylish pillows. Locally found antlers from elk and mule deer decorate the walls. An old wagon wheel fitted with six glass shades makes a unique chandelier.

FACING: Another of the kids' guest bedrooms offers built-in "cubbyhole" beds. The colorful bedding adds a sense of energy and playfulness to the room.

RIGHT: This small guest bedroom offers a pair of single beds. The simple yet colorful quilted bedding along with minimal use of decorative objects creates a restful setting for guests. The massive doors were created from historic barn beams.

ABOVE, LEFT: A massive bathtub complete with claw feet occupies the kids' bathroom on the second floor. Industrial faucets add to the setting and a vintage Navajo carpet from the Ganado region completes the room.

ABOVE, RIGHT: This bath offers a marble top on the vanity and stylized gold faucets. The custom doors were designed by Larry Pearson. A small three-light antler chandelier and wall sconces light the room.

LEFT: On the opposite wall of the kids' bath rests this sink with three faucets. The basin is metal and the vanity was made from recycled barn beams.

The home sits at a very high level and has the appearance of
looking like it has been on the site for generations.

THE Pointe

Sitting on an outcrop that offers views that have to be seen to be believed, The Pointe, as it is called, occupies a site that is also the home to moose, elk, bears and mountain goats. It's not an easy place to find and it is advisable to have a four-wheel drive vehicle during any season when visiting the home. Occupying more than nine thousand square feet, the home offers seven bedrooms and seven baths. It was designed by Larry Pearson and built by Lohss Construction. Carole Young of Carole Young Design, Southport, Connecticut, served as the interior designer.

PREVIOUS OVERLEAF: Larry Pearson often incorporates horizon lines and forms inherent in the local environment into his designs. The roof is covered with shake shingles.

ABOVE, LEFT: The front door of the home was hand made from recycled materials. The rugged nature of the door adds to the character of the home.

ABOVE, RIGHT: The custom doors throughout most of the home offer a variety of geometric designs and patterns.

ABOVE: The home offers a minimalist approach to interior design. Here a single print by Andy Warhol fills the hallway.

RIGHT: A pair of massive rustic cabinets greets visitors to the home and provides storage space for cold weather garments.

LEFT: The main living room offers a floor-to-ceiling fireplace and comfortable upholstered furniture.

FACING, ABOVE: An overview of the living room shows the floor-to-ceiling fireplace, built-in nooks, balcony railing and furniture.

FACING, BELOW: The living room offers a number of upholstered pieces of furniture. The color of the fabric brings life to the setting.

ABOVE, LEFT: An industrial strength range with a custom steel and iron hood tickle a cook's fancy. The countertops are granite.

ABOVE, RIGHT: The kitchen has not only a fireplace but also a marble island complete with built-in appliances and sink. The island top is Calacatta marble. The three custom hanging chandeliers are from Ann Morris of New York.

FACING: The pantry off the kitchen offers country styling, plenty of cabinet space and granite countertops.

FACING: The main dining room also offers a fireplace. The artwork over the mantel is by Dubuffet. The 1960s chandelier is by British designer Anthony Redmile.

ABOVE: A custom walnut "Salamanca" dining table from Dos Gallos is surrounded by ten Spanish Colonial dining chairs covered with Edelman leather. The ceiling and doors for the built-in wall cabinets are lined with birch bark. The floor is covered with slabs of stone. Large windows allow the room to fill with light and also provide great views of the surrounding environment.

LEFT: A wine cellar sits behind the staircase in the ground floor of the home.

ABOVE: Massive materials were often used throughout the home to create staircases, beds, railings and other architectural elements.

FACING, ABOVE: The upstairs balcony is outlined by a railing system made of lodgepole pine. The massive chandelier was created from iron and elk antlers by Arden Creek Designs.

FACING, BELOW: The second-floor balcony has recycled wide pine boards as flooring. Custom bookcases sit on either side of the windows, and a pair of club chairs covered with cowhide offers a quiet spot to peruse the literature.

FACING: An upstairs nook offers a rustic chair made from moose antlers.
An original Warhol print hangs on the wall above the chair.

ABOVE: A small area on the second floor serves as a playroom for kids. Here
built-in window seats and a flat-screen TV are the central features.

LEFT: The master bedroom offers a massive bed with a headboard inlaid with half-round antlers. The bench at the foot of the bed has legs made from elk antlers and a leather top. The carpet is from The Rug Company in London and New York. The 1960s crystal chandelier has bubble-shaped prisms.

FACING: An upstairs study off the master bedroom offers a single leather club chair and ottoman. The room is illuminated by an Arts and Crafts chandelier and an industrial design floor lamp.

FACING: The master bath offers walls of stone and recycled wood. A half-dome chandelier lights the room.

RIGHT: A lengthy soaking tub inset into a rock wall is the main feature of the master bath. Shelves on the wall provide space for candles and other bath accessories.

FACING: A pair of upstairs bedrooms offers built-in rustic bunk beds. Made of highly organic, twisted material, the rooms are the delight of visitors. The metal chandelier is lined with mica.

ABOVE, LEFT: Another view of one of the bunk rooms.

ABOVE, RIGHT: The bunk rooms also contain built-in beds for overflow guests.

RIGHT: The bathroom between the bunk rooms offers a two-faucet cast-iron sink and a vanity made from half-round branches.

LEFT: This headboard was created from a massive branch of lodgepole pine. The star-shaped glass chandeliers make this a dreamer's delight.

FACING: The home boasts clean lines and well-placed accessories. This bedroom has a built-in window seat and subtle artwork. The subdued window treatments complement the massive logs throughout the home.

FACING: A massive bed in an upstairs room is supported by flared stumps as posts. The fireplace makes it a welcoming retreat.

RIGHT: Built-in cabinets are often found in the bedrooms and other areas of the home.

ABOVE, LEFT: Massive recycled beams made from lodgepole pine trees provide the supporting materials for the staircase and downstairs recreation area.

ABOVE, RIGHT: The downstairs recreation room boasts a bar with a copper top on the service area and a number of tall bar stools.

FACING, ABOVE: The recreation room contains a built-in flat-screen TV. The couches are covered with antique Turkish Kilim carpets.

FACING, BELOW: The stunning pool table is the Naragansett model designed in the 1860s by H. W. Collender. A bearskin rug rests under the pool table.

TWO EAGLE
Ranch

The directions seemed simple enough. Drive toward the morning sun, turn right at the big oak tree, turn left at each fork in the road, the house is at the base of the mountain, last place when it dead ends. The number of the home was even given, as was the name of the street, which now eludes me. So off we went. It was just another adventure for my ten-year-old daughter, my wife and me. Two hours later we were on the correct dirt road, and after some consternation and heated discussion, we finally found the proper turnoff. The dust clouds behind our vehicle announced to the entire world that we were arriving.

After many anxious minutes we found a fence and a driveway having the correct address. The structures on the land included an old barn, a chicken coop and a tool shed. A small, old log cabin, presently under rehabilitation, was also evident. I parked the car and walked onto the property. It was not at all what I expected or was led to believe. It was certainly not a significant, innovative compound or structure. Without much thought I knocked on the cabin door and called, hoping that someone was present. No one answered. Five minutes later I walked casually back to the car. Once I had the car running and in gear, I noticed someone walking toward us. After greeting the gentleman I was invited to see the home. And after walking through the two-bedroom building I will admit to being a bit disappointed. But after a few minutes the gentleman finally said, "I guess you want to see the main house." And after laughing a bit, he called the owner of the home and announced our arrival.

The main house, the one we had come to photograph, was another mile or so up what can only be described as a goat path. Traveling slowly along the trail we passed trout ponds filled with rising fish, a dozen or so deer, antelopes and brilliant aspen trees in fall color. As we ascended the foothills of the mountain the full impact of the ranch became clear: the entire place was nothing less than stunning.

The owner invited us to hop onto a pair of four-wheeler ATVs to get a tour of the property. Having never driven an ATV, I was quite proud of myself as I maneuvered the vehicle along the paths. But with my daughter frantically clinging to my back, I nearly toppled it on a steep incline as we climbed a high ridge. Regardless, we had a great time!

We finally reached the summit and before us were many thousands of acres of absolute wilderness. The owner casually mentioned that the property was also home to grizzly and black bears, wolves, cougars, moose and other animals as well. And almost nightly, a herd of a few hundred elk grazed on one of the pastures very near the home.

PREVIOUS OVERLEAF, LEFT: Nestled comfortably into the foothills of the Rocky Mountains just above Yellowstone National Park, the home is surrounded by aspen and lodgepole pine trees.

PREVIOUS OVERLEAF, RIGHT: The roof of Two Eagle Ranch is covered with cold rolled steel. The outer layer of the material rusts quickly and adds to the historical, "been there forever" look.

Another Larry Pearson project, the design is a subtle, contemporary effort. Innovative in many ways, the building was to become both a ranch and a family home. The young couple empowered and encouraged Pearson to both innovate and respect the wilderness on which the home was to reside. With that said, the 7,500-square-foot home is a subtle place complete with unexpected design and construction amenities. A blend of metal and wood, it offers knee braces, exposed I-beams, flanges and countertops all made from steel. A massive central stone fireplace on one end of the building is complemented by a second, floor-to-ceiling fireplace on the opposite end of the great room. The main bedroom and guest wing are on opposite sides of the building and dramatic views are apparent from any window in the home. The atmosphere and ambiance invite visitors to kick off their shoes and relax.

The owners of the ranch were very instrumental in the design and interiors of the home. The building was constructed by Langlas & Associates of Billings and Bozeman. The art was provided by the design firm of Betsy Swartz, also of Bozeman. Hill Masonry of Billings was responsible for the fireplaces and the stonework throughout the project.

The extra-wide front door was custom made from old barn beams.
The hinges and window frame were fabricated from steel.

FACING: The great room for Two Eagle Ranch offers several sitting areas as well as fireplaces on opposite ends. The floor is outlined with concrete, with recycled boards inlaid in the center, high-use area of the room. Radiant heat warms the building. Steel detailing includes knee braces, exposed I-beams and flanges, evident throughout the room. The large chandeliers, created by Ambiance of Bozeman, are lined with mica and create a warm glow.

RIGHT: The fireplaces in the ranch were constructed of Harlowton stone quarried from the nearby pits in Harlowton, Montana. Barn beams supported by steel braces make the fireplace mantel.

FACING: Another view of the great room shows oversized leather armchairs and ottomans. The white cabinet beneath the windows houses a large-screen TV that rises on the push of a button. The colorful carpet in the foreground adds energy to the room.

ABOVE: Steel turnbuckles were incorporated into the staircase system and are consistent with the other exposed structural steel elements in the home. The art throughout is traditional western motif.

RIGHT: A pair of "designer" chairs with scrolled arms rest up against the wall. The concrete floor was stained brown to blend with the interior of the home. The art on the back wall was provided by Betsy Swartz.

LEFT: The kitchen at Two Eagle Ranch offers a custom-made island surrounded by hickory bar stools. The range hood, shelves and countertops are all steel. The range, admits the owner, is too small to cook turkeys at Thanksgiving, so they have chicken and Cornish hens.

FACING: A custom picnic table and benches serve as a dining spot for impromptu meals. The cabinet on the right houses the refrigerator. Dark brown cement floors blend with the setting and are easily cleaned.

FACING, ABOVE: The master bedroom occupies one wing of the home and has an outside balcony from which to watch the elk feeding in the evenings.

FACING, BELOW: A pair of twin antique iron beds occupies one of the guest rooms. The artwork was provided by Betsy Swartz.

ABOVE, LEFT: The bunk room offers a twin over a double bed.

ABOVE, RIGHT: This bath has a marble countertop and accessories. The walls are covered with square-cut tiles of leather.

ABOVE: A full-size antique iron bed with plaid pillows and an antique
geometric quilt provides for guests in one of several bedrooms.

FACING: This bathroom sink offers custom cabinetry made from recycled materials
and a hammered copper sink. Western artifacts complement the setting.

FACING: A sitting room in the guest wing offers a massive fireplace and four comfortable leather armchairs surrounding a circular coffee table. A variety of western collectibles enhances the setting.

ABOVE: The outside cooking area, complete with picnic table, Adirondack chairs, and cooking stations, offers dramatic views of the foothills.

WHITEFISH *Retreat*

Whitefish Retreat is a stunning lakeside home that features four different levels. Built on a very narrow, steep lot, the home includes several bedrooms, living and dining room, great porches and stunning views. It's an unpretentious home where I felt perfectly comfortable taking off my shoes, having a glass of wine and watching the flames burn down in the fireplace.

Photographing the exterior of the home was no easy task. All of the boats had been put away for the winter and although the dock was still in place, it did not extend out far enough into the lake to allow me to photograph the building in its entirety. In time, fortunately, I was able to wave down an individual on a jet ski. This person was kind enough to allow

PREVIOUS OVERLEAF, LEFT: As evening settles in, the colors of the sky soften. Although windy most of the day, the air came to a standstill and allowed the water to become perfectly still. As seen from the hill above the home, the dramatic views become apparent.

PREVIOUS OVERLEAF, RIGHT: Shake shingles cover the multilevel roof and one end of a room exterior. Board and batten siding covers the rest.

LEFT: The massive front door was custom made from rugged ancient timbers. An Arts and Crafts ceiling fixture lights the foyer.

FACING: The kitchen island has a built-in wine cooler. Comfortable, contemporary barstools line the island.

me to hop on the back of her vehicle and motored me a few hundred yards out into the lake. And even though I was soaked from the ride I got the picture!

Constructed by Ebbett Builders, the home was engineered by Beaudette Consulting Engineers of Montana, with Carole Hamill and Associates as the interior design firm.

LEFT: Designed in the Arts and Crafts style, the kitchen is complete with built-in ovens and custom cabinetry. The door with the leaded glass insets leads to the pantry.

FACING, ABOVE: The kitchen offers an island with built-in range. The countertops are soapstone.

FACING: A two-drawer table holding a lamp made of an old log sits in a small nook off the kitchen area. The cabinet to the right houses the freezer and refrigerator.

ABOVE: The dining room offers this custom sawbuck table surrounded by eight side chairs. An Arts and Crafts ceiling fixture overhangs the table. The floors throughout the home are recycled barn boards. A custom wall divider complete with doors and storage space separates the dining from the living room.

FACING, ABOVE: This 1950s-style lounge set resides in one of the several rooms overlooking the lake.

FACING, BELOW: The living room, adjacent to the kitchen, offers a large fireplace, wicker armchairs, upholstered sofas and a contrasting carpet on the floor. An Arts and Crafts chandelier hangs from the ceiling.

ABOVE: Leading to the lower level, this staircase was created from rough-cut pine. Iron spindles support the two banisters. The massive lower level of the fireplace offers recessed shelving for collectibles such as the antique ship's lantern shown here.

FACING: The downstairs bunk room is a favorite of the kids. The flush-mounted chandelier is nothing more than an old bucket turned upside down!

ABOVE: This custom vanity is complete with a granite countertop and stone door pulls. The sink and faucets are stainless steel.

RIGHT: The downstairs bath offers a custom rustic vanity with applied birch bark on the doors. The sinks are porcelain and the countertop is a thick slab of recycled wood.

FACING: The downstairs recreation area contains comfortable upholstered furniture as well as a complete wet bar and custom cabinets. The front of the bar island is covered with half-round logs, and the countertop is soapstone.

RIGHT: A massive fireplace, oriental carpet and wicker furniture occupy an enclosed back porch. The chandelier was created from bunches of twigs wrapped around a center fixture. A small wooden canoe filled with pine cones rests on the mantel.

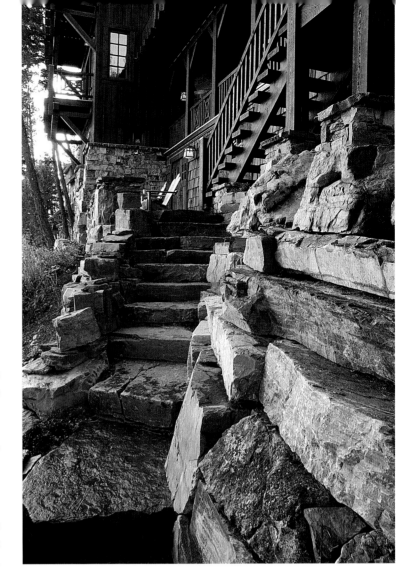

FACING: Seen from the lake are the home's four levels, a variety of porches, a massive fireplace and extensive stonework.

RIGHT: The property had to be re-contoured to allow for construction of the building and landscaping. The back staircase is complete with massive rocks.

BELOW: One level of the back porch system provides space for this outdoor dining set with a glass-top table and a full working fireplace.

THE
Hideaway

They found the lot advertised in the *New York Times* and bought it immediately. Located an hour outside of New York City, the property is an absolute mecca. Surrounded by hundreds of acres of preserve, this home is a gem in the wilderness.

The design started as a rough sketch by Larry Pearson on a napkin. It quickly evolved to what it is today. The owners of the property, a passionate couple with superb taste, were involved in every detail of the design and construction. Not only did they help refine the details of the drawings but they were intimately involved with materials selection and the interior design. They wanted the structure to offer character, warmth and charm, and they sought only the finest materials for the construction of their home.

The owners experimented with a variety of chemical processes—such as fuming, boiled linseed oil and turpentine, and shellac—to develop the richest colors for the finishes on their furniture and interiors. And it wasn't easy. Ultimately, they wound up being their own general contractor, overseeing every detail of the completion of the building. The home was built by Mark Conese of Easton, Connecticut. The massive fireplace rests on a huge six-foot-by-eight-foot concrete slab. An exterior fireplace shares a common chimney system, and a second interior fireplace occupies the master bedroom. Ken Uracius of Stone & Lime Imports, Holden, Massachusetts, was responsible for the fireplaces and other masonry throughout the home. Metal artist Joe Holley was responsible for the lighting, firescreen and fire tools. Most of the furniture was custom made. The cabinetry throughout was created by David Bartlett Woodworking of Easton, Connecticut. The logs for the home were imported from the Rocky Mountains, and most of the floors were created from recycled materials. The intricate log scribing, post and beam work and flooring were done by the talented artistic team of Julio Gomez, John Blocker and Miguel Gomez.

An adjacent building serves as a garage and storage facility, with an upstairs apartment that acts as quarters for guests. The 4,500-square-foot home has six bedrooms.

The owners were passionate about the environment and made a significant commitment to insuring that the home blended with the surroundings. A lengthy dirt road complete with ruts, bumps and overgrown vegetation extends right up to the front door. Two ponds naturalize the setting, and the indigenous surrounding of the property was carefully restored.

In truth, this is a grand place! When the leaves are in full fall color or the home is covered with a thick blanket of snow, it is absolutely spectacular! It's pretty nice in the summer too.

PREVIOUS OVERLEAF, LEFT: Approaching the home in the autumn visitors are treated to a variety of hues. The home offers a main building, garage with upstairs apartment and a connecting breezeway.

ABOVE: A handmade, solid oak door created from recycled boards serves as the entranceway to the home. The doors throughout the home were handcrafted by John DeLuca. The ceiling in the foyer is lined with birch bark. The ornate entryway table was created by Randy Holden and the painting and frame are from the artistic hands of Veronica Nemethy.

RIGHT: Tucked away in the corner of the ceiling is this striking, hand-carved owl in attack position. The owl was created by Jason Tennant.

ABOVE: The great room at The Hideaway offers both warmth and character. The lodgepole pine logs for the home were imported from Montana. The dramatic fireplace was designed by Larry Pearson and was executed by mason Ken Uracius. Joe Holley completed the massive chandelier and other lighting for the home. The flooring consists of recycled barn boards.

FACING: A closer view offers the details of the fireplace. The firescreen, andirons and fire tools were handcrafted by Joe Holley.

RIGHT: The powder room off the great room offers this rustic washbasin. The stump is peeled cedar and the sink is hammered copper. The faucets are also copper.

BELOW: The sweeping curves of the sofa offer a sense of casualness and relaxation to the setting. The coffee table is from the Ralph Kylloe Gallery.

FACING: As in many homes, the kitchen is the hub of this house. Oak bar stools provide seating around the island. Soapstone was used for the countertops and also as the backsplash behind the sink. Metalsmith Joe Holley created the hood for the range. The island and cabinets were created by David Bartlett.

RIGHT: Complete with numerous drawers and cupboards for storage space, the kitchen island also contains an industrial strength range. The island is made of recycled barn beams.

FACING: A set of bow-back Windsor chairs surrounds the formal dining table. The table was made by John Blokker. An upright piano from the 1920s rests against the wall. Joe Holley created the chandelier over the dining table.

ABOVE: In a small area of the kitchen, an art deco table lamp sits on top of a mint-condition stereo phonograph from the 1950s. A flat-screen TV is attached to the wall.

RIGHT: A small sitting area off the kitchen offers a stump-base table made from maple and a variety of green plants.

LEFT: The master bedroom also offers a floor-to-ceiling fireplace. An antique quilt covers the sleigh bed and a pair of owl andirons occupies the fireplace.

ABOVE: The master bath and dressing room offer Oriental styling. The clean lines of this storage unit are indicative of the sense of simplicity sought by the owners of the home.

ABOVE: The golden, vertical tiles in the shower room resemble bamboo.

RIGHT: The master bath also offers a clear view of the backyard. The bath windows open, allowing fresh breezes to fill the room. The waterspout for the bath is actually a hollow piece of bamboo.

FACING, ABOVE: A southern view of the home shows the attached porch, which is used frequently throughout the year.

FACING, BELOW: The covered back porch extends to an open area and offers a pair of Adirondack chairs to view the sunsets.

ABOVE, LEFT: A walk through the breezeway lined with bark-on cedar trees allows another view of the setting.

ABOVE, RIGHT: The back of the home offers a quiet garden area complete with a round stone table, comfortable armchairs and an outdoor cooker.

FACING, ABOVE: Guests are invited to relax and enjoy the dramatic view from the covered back porch. Comfortable Bar Harbor wicker chairs provide seating to watch the fall colors and sunsets.

FACING, BELOW: One needs to be reminded that this setting of pink skies and peaceful valleys is only an hour north of the hustle and bustle of New York City.

ABOVE: Facing west, the home offers grand views of sunsets from a rustic back porch.

Resources

ARCHITECT

LARRY PEARSON, ARCHITECT
777 East Main St., Ste. 203
Bozeman, MT 59715-3809
406.587.1997
www.pearsondesigngroup.com

BUILDERS/CONTRACTORS/ SUPPLIERS

AUTHENTIC MONTANA HOMES
Michael D. Casey
PO Box 314
McAllister, MT 59740
406.682.7266

C.F. CONSTRUCTION
Mark Conese
PO Box 54
Easton, CT 06612
203.550.5753
markc@optonline.net

EBBETT BUILDERS
534 Columbia Ave.
Whitefish, MT 59937
406.862.3439

JOE HOLLEY, BLACKSMITH/METALSMITH
189 Woodard Rd.
Fort Edward, NY 12828
Home 518.638.5702
Cell 518.321.4128
hmp12828@yahoo.com

LANGLAS & ASSOCIATES
2270 Grant Rd.
Billings, MT 59102
406.656.0629

777 E. Main St., Ste. 101
Bozeman, MT 59715
406.551.6699
www.langlas.com

LOHSS CONSTRUCTION
77150 Gallatin Rd.
Bozeman, MT 59718-9177
www.lohssconstruction.com
406.763.9081

ON SITE MANAGEMENT
417 W. Mendenhall
Bozeman, MT 59715
406.586.1500
www.onsitemanagement.com

SANDOVAL MASONRY INC
77090 Gallatin Road Apt. A
Bozeman, MT 59718
Office 406.763.4765
Fax 406.763.4750
Cell 406.570.6027
www.sandovalmasonry.com

YELLOWSTONE TRADITIONS
34290 E. Frontage Rd
Bozeman, MT 59715-8625
406.587.0968
www.yellowstonetraditions.com

INTERIOR DESIGNERS

BETSY SWARTZ FINE ART CONSULTING, INC.
2000 Fairway Dr., Ste. 105
Bozeman, MT 59715
406.585.8339
betsy@betsyswartzfineart.com
www.betsyswartzfineart.com

CAROLE YOUNG DESIGN
PO Box 111
Southport, CT 06890
203.254.5656
caroleyoungdesign@gmail.com

CAROLE HAMILL & ASSOCIATES
16119 Chalfont Circle
Dallas, TX 95248
972.239.9385

DPS INTERIORS
Charles de Lisle
643 7th St.
San Francisco, CA 94103
415.565.6767

ELIZABETH SCHULTZ, DESIGNWORKS
19 W. Babcock St.
Bozeman, MT 59715
406.582.0222

HILARY HEMINWAY INTERIORS
140 Briarpatch Rd.
Stonington, CT 06378
860.535.3110

PAUL FERRANTE, INC.
Pacific Design Center
8464 Melrose Pl., Ste. B-362
Los Angeles, CA 90069
310.854.4412
www.paulferrante.com

PEACE DESIGN
349 Peachtree Hills Ave. NE C2
Atlanta, GA 30305
404.237.8681
Fax 404.237.6150
www.peacedesign.org

SECRET GARDEN INTERIORS
Jeanne Jenkins
5612 Mooretown Rd.
Williamsburg, VA 23188
757.220.8477
www.secretgardeninteriors.com

CIVIL ENGINEERING COMPANIES

BEAUDETTE CONSULTING ENGINEERS, INC.
131 W. Main St.
Missoula, MT 59802
406.721.7315
www.bceweb.com

BRIDGER ENGINEERS, INC
2233 W. Kagy Blvd., Ste. 3
Bozeman, MT 59718
406.585.0590
www.bridgerengineers.com

FURNITURE GALLERIES

DAVIS-TORRES COLLECTION
128 E. Main St.
Bozeman, MT 59715
406.587.1587

MONTANA TRAILS GALLERY
402 E. Main St.
Bozeman, MT 59715
406.586.2166
Fax 406.586.2106
steve@montanatrails.com

RALPH KYLLOE GALLERY
PO Box 669
Lake George, NY 12845
518.696.4100
www.ralphkylloe.com
info@ralphkylloe.com

TIERNEY FINE ART
127 E. Main St.
Bozeman, MT 59715-4761
406.586.4521
www.tierneyfineart.com

FURNITURE BUILDERS AND SUPPLIERS

ADIRONDACK AUDIO AND VIDEO
Mike Timko
1048 State Rt. 9
Queensbury, NY 12804
518.792.3528
mtimko@adkav.com
www.adkav.com

AMBIANCE
81211 Gallatin Rd.
Bozeman, MT 59718-5968
406.585.2276

ARTS & CRAFTS HARDWARE
Gerry Rucks
28011 Malvina Dr.
Warren, MI 48088-4322
586.772.7279
www.arts-n-craftshardware.com

DAVID BARTLETT FINE CUSTOM
CABINETRY AND FURNITURE
Easton, CT 06612
203.268.9408
www.davidbartlettwoodworking.com

FIRE MOUNTAIN FORGE
1 West End Rd.
Livingston, MT 59047
406.222.9732
www.firemountainforge.com
info@firemountainforge.com

MARC TAGGART & COMPANY
1735 E. Sheridan, Ste. 217
Cody, WY 82414
Office 307.587.1800
Cell 307.899.9381
marc@marctaggart.com

SANTOS FURNITURE
Lester Santos
PO Box 176
Cody, WY 82414
1.888.woodguy
www.lestersantos.com

TODD GARDENIER WORKS (TGW)
PO Box 6682
Bozeman, MT 59718
Office 406.994.0800
Cell 406.580.6726
Fax 406.994.9102

TIM GROTH FURNITURE
PO Box 12
Jackson, WY 83001
208.870.9938
timgroth@timgrothfurniture.com

WOOD RIVER RUSTICS
Doug Tedrow
PO Box 3446
Ketchum, ID 83340
208.726.1442

OWNER'S REPRESENTATIVE

SAVANTAGE
William W. Callahan
406.579.4896
Fax 406.624.6379
wcallahan@savantagecr.com

PAINTING/PLASTERING

ESMOND LYONS FINE ART AND
DECORATIVE PAINTING
13 Garfield St.
Glens Falls, NY 12801
518.307.6665

H & S WALL SYSTEMS
Brett Harrell
1739 Remuda Dr.
Belgrade, MT 59714
Office 406.388.1927
Cell 406.579.6230

MALLON PLASTERING, INC.
Jeremy "Scooter" Mallon
2350 Shatto Dr.
Belgrade, MT 59714
Office 406.388.2627
Cell 406.599.8556
Mallonplastering@q.com